Celebration of Life

When I come to thue end of the day,

And the sun has set for me.

I want no rites in a gloom-filled room.

Why cry for a soul set free?

Miss me a little, but not too long,

And not with your head bowed low.

Remember the love we once shared –

Miss me, but let me go.

For this is a journey we all must take,

And each must go alone.

It's all part of the maker's plan,

A step on road to home.

When you are lonely and sick at heart

Go to the friends we know.

And bury your sorrows in doing good deeds –

Miss me, but let me go.

In Memory of

....

....

....

....

Guest's Name

Thoughts & Memories

....

....

....

....

....

....

....

....

....

....

....

....

....

....

....

Guest's Name

Thoughts & Memories

Guest's Name

Thoughts & Memories

Guest's Name

Thoughts & Memories

....

....

....

....

....

....

....

....

....

....

....

....

Guest's Name

Thoughts & Memories

Guest's Name

Thoughts & Memories

....

....

....

....

....

....

....

....

....

....

....

....

Guest's Name

Thoughts & Memories

Guest's Name

Thoughts & Memories

Guest's Name

Thoughts & Memories

Guest's Name

Thoughts & Memories

Guest's Name

Thoughts & Memories

Guest's Name

....

....

....

....

....

....

....

....

Thoughts & Memories

....

....

....

....

....

....

....

....

....

....

....

....

Guest's Name

Thoughts & Memories

Guest's Name

Thoughts & Memories

Guest's Name

Thoughts & Memories

Guest's Name

Thoughts & Memories

Guest's Name

Thoughts & Memories

Guest's Name

Thoughts & Memories

Guest's Name

Thoughts & Memories

Guest's Name

Thoughts & Memories

Guest's Name

Thoughts & Memories

Guest's Name

Thoughts & Memories

Guest's Name

Thoughts & Memories

Guest's Name

Thoughts & Memories

Guest's Name

Thoughts & Memories

Guest's Name

....

....

....

....

....

....

....

Thoughts & Memories

....

....

....

....

....

....

....

....

....

....

....

....

Guest's Name

Thoughts & Memories

Guest's Name

Thoughts & Memories

Guest's Name

Thoughts & Memories

Guest's Name

Thoughts & Memories

Guest's Name

Thoughts & Memories

Guest's Name

....

....

....

....

....

....

....

Thoughts & Memories

....

....

....

....

....

....

....

....

....

....

....

....

Guest's Name

Thoughts & Memories

Guest's Name

Thoughts & Memories

Guest's Name

Thoughts & Memories

Guest's Name

Thoughts & Memories

Guest's Name

Thoughts & Memories

Guest's Name

Thoughts & Memories

Guest's Name

Thoughts & Memories

Guest's Name

Thoughts & Memories

Guest's Name

Thoughts & Memories

....

....

....

....

....

....

....

....

Guest's Name

Thoughts & Memories

Guest's Name

Thoughts & Memories

Guest's Name

Thoughts & Memories

Guest's Name

Thoughts & Memories

Guest's Name

Thoughts & Memories

Guest's Name

Thoughts & Memories

Guest's Name

Thoughts & Memories

Guest's Name

Thoughts & Memories

Guest's Name

Thoughts & Memories

Guest's Name

Thoughts & Memories

Guest's Name

Thoughts & Memories

Guest's Name

Thoughts & Memories

Guest's Name

Thoughts & Memories

Guest's Name

Thoughts & Memories

Guest's Name

Thoughts & Memories

Guest's Name

Thoughts & Memories

Guest's Name

Thoughts & Memories

Guest's Name

Thoughts & Memories

Guest's Name

Thoughts & Memories

....

....

....

....

....

....

....

....

....

....

....

....

....

....

....

....

....

....

....

....

....

....

Guest's Name

Thoughts & Memories

Guest's Name

....

....

....

....

....

....

....

....

Thoughts & Memories

....

....

....

....

....

....

....

....

....

....

....

....

Guest's Name

Thoughts & Memories

Guest's Name

Thoughts & Memories

Guest's Name

Thoughts & Memories

Guest's Name

Thoughts & Memories

Guest's Name

Thoughts & Memories

Guest's Name

....

....

....

....

....

....

....

Thoughts & Memories

....

....

....

....

....

....

....

....

....

....

....

....

....

Guest's Name

Thoughts & Memories

Guest's Name

....

....

....

....

....

....

....

....

Thoughts & Memories

....

....

....

....

....

....

....

....

....

....

....

....

Guest's Name

Thoughts & Memories

Guest's Name

Thoughts & Memories

Guest's Name

Thoughts & Memories

Guest's Name

Thoughts & Memories

Guest's Name

Thoughts & Memories

Guest's Name

Thoughts & Memories

Guest's Name

Thoughts & Memories

Guest's Name

Thoughts & Memories

Guest's Name

Thoughts & Memories

Guest's Name

Thoughts & Memories

Guest's Name

Thoughts & Memories

Guest's Name

Thoughts & Memories

Guest's Name

Thoughts & Memories

Guest's Name

Thoughts & Memories

....

....

....

....

....

....

....

....

....

....

....

....

....

....

....

....

....

....

....

....

....

Guest's Name

Thoughts & Memories

Guest's Name

Thoughts & Memories

Guest's Name

Thoughts & Memories

Guest's Name

Thoughts & Memories

Guest's Name

Thoughts & Memories

Guest's Name

....

....

....

....

....

....

....

Thoughts & Memories

....

....

....

....

....

....

....

....

....

....

....

....

Guest's Name

Thoughts & Memories

Guest's Name

Thoughts & Memories

Guest's Name

Thoughts & Memories

Guest's Name

Thoughts & Memories

Guest's Name

Thoughts & Memories

Guest's Name

Thoughts & Memories

Guest's Name

Thoughts & Memories

Guest's Name

Thoughts & Memories

....

....

....

....

Guest's Name

Thoughts & Memories

Guest's Name

Thoughts & Memories

Guest's Name

Thoughts & Memories

Guest's Name

Thoughts & Memories

Guest's Name

Thoughts & Memories

Guest's Name

Thoughts & Memories

Guest's Name

Thoughts & Memories

Guest's Name

Thoughts & Memories

Guest's Name

Thoughts & Memories

Guest's Name

....

....

....

....

....

....

....

....

Thoughts & Memories

....

....

....

....

....

....

....

....

....

....

....

....

Guest's Name

Thoughts & Memories

Guest's Name

Thoughts & Memories

Guest's Name

Thoughts & Memories

Guest's Name

Thoughts & Memories